Flesh Enough

Poems

Darla Himeles

Get Fresh Books, LLC
Union, New Jersey

Get Fresh Books, LLC
PO BOX 901
Union, New Jersey 07083

www.getfreshbooksllc.com

ISBN: 978-0-9989358-0-5

Cover image: "The Back Yard" from *All Circus Around Us*, courtesy of Dawn Surratt

Cover design & book layout: Leonardo Zuñiga

Author photo: Jessica White

Acknowledgments

I'm grateful to the editors of the following journals for publishing poems from this chapbook, sometimes in earlier versions:

Eclipse: A Literary Journal—"Cousin"
Naugatuck River Review—"On the Runaway Angus Bull the Stewarts Kindly Saved"
Pittsburgh Poetry Review—"In the Beginning"
Women's Review of Books—"On the Day Adrienne Rich Died"

"They'll Say the Blue Whale's Tongue Weighed As Much As an Elephant" was selected by ARTS by the People for the Moving Words Project. An animated short film by Ron Levin based on my poem is published online.

Contents

for my mother, Barbara Ann

Flesh Enough

They'll Say the Blue Whale's Tongue Weighed As Much As an Elephant

Someday your daughter
will voice this fact
and ask

what an elephant was like

and you will find her
sunbaked tires
to pet

and heavy bovine leathers
and summer earth
whose anthills pulse

and you will bring her photos
of a trunk spiraled round
a paint-dipped brush

or splashing pond water
into an open mouth

and you will run with palm leaves
catching wind on either side
of your head

and rock the arc of your body
over couch cushions
to show how rescuers grunted

CPR in Bee Gees rhythm
on the last baby elephant,
his mother gone before him,

and your daughter will sketch
elephants from old books
and ask what they smelled like,

whether their stomachs were softer
than their backs.

You'll swerve back to the weight
of an elephant, how even an elephant
eleven months with child

equaled but the tongue of the blue whale,
whose heft sung the fathoms.

But what if she asks the weight
of the blue whale's voice?
How will you give her a song

that swelled the sea? A heart the size
of a Volkswagen, pounding?

Redolence

Is redolence passed?
Those who never slept
under an almond tree's branch

might not catch almond blossoms
on a breeze—
even if their grandmothers dreamt
by the Dead Sea.

I, too, born beyond Babylon—
who never knew bitter almond
crept through the vents

as my ancestors showered in gas—
might not taste almond's breath
sour-sweet in a morning kiss.

Chaya Speaks

Call me Chaya Devorah,
        liveliest honeybee.

Call me Shylock,
        the spat upon—
        yea, prick this flesh, we both
        bleed.

These breasts burst myrrh,
        these braids trap lavender,
        & into the venomous mouth, I vomit
        honey.

Call me Shulamith, dark
        horse racing the pasture,
        hooves cutting earth against
        erasure.

C&D Canal, August 2008
for Betsy

Dredged dust, sneaker-stirred, births fossilized belemnite
rostra, amber bullets modern squid evolved away from,

but in your hands, they're delicate as daisies,
good for braiding with tussock sedge into a crown

I'd wed you under tomorrow, or next summer. For you,
ancient sea creatures slap long-vanished flesh

against dusty shins, squid legs flutter like blackgum
leaves in autumn fog. As light quakes the chestnuts free

of your eye, the soft rattle of Delaware's cephalopod dead
kisses my palms—our bodies hold this Late Cretaceous love song.

Tweet

Shadowed—passenger pigeons'
cacophonous noontime
endarkenment—slave food,
down comforters, billions carnaged
til Martha, captive, the last

Manatee

Near Florida currents,
        I laid careful fingers
in his back's propeller-cut grooves,
           pressed my feet into the tough
spatula of his tail, and rambled
        about rotten pomegranates,
salt-water-soaked wheat,
        shattered wine glasses
on sticky linoleum floor.
        We wept and laughed
over humankind's foolishness,
        his two eyes
cataracted by microplastics.

Flesh Enough

The body dense with death
cannot be lifted by the shadow
of our arms, we who never knew
the live body's particular song,
our arms slipping beneath the flesh,
our arms useless in not-blood-pool,
not-prison, not-police-van—the shadow
of our arms slipping beneath the flesh
of Trayvon Martin, of Sandra Bland,
of Michael Brown, of Sarah Lee Circle Bear,
of
of   —
if we believe the mind has arms,
if we believe the mind has arms
flesh enough to lift the body.

On the Day Adrienne Rich Died

I woke with a headache   read Ginsberg on the couch two hours
orange tabby beneath palm   waiting on aspirin

then rose   watched snow wet the deck

I sat at my desk   marked student essays on Sappho
read a few times a poem in the New Yorker   called "Truth"

Came in my hands after lunch   I was greener than grass

Snow started to stick by dinner: my wife's quinoa & black beans
her stories from her day my stories   as the sky darkened

Our eyes: tired crescent moons across the table

When my sister texted the news   I stood beneath the darkening sky
with cracked tongue   taste of ash

        how her words startled my eyes open

        how the night caught in my throat

9

Cousin

You will never rip apart the challah,
warm and wrapped in Malaysian linen,

while my wife holds the other end
in our home.

When we met, your back
locked; between your vertebrae

are traditions I have craved,

secretly kissing mezuzahs in doorways
and stumbling through the sh'ma alone.

Our pots and pans are spoiled, cousin, with sins
I don't believe in, and when I bleed,

I touch everything.

Fuchsia

Whole years lumber sometimes
heavy-footed, un-poachable,
encircled by armed guards

like the last male northern white
rhino, until the thick knees
buckle and the beast bows

to beige earth. Sometimes
silence breathes heavy
between siblings. She tells me
she never took out the trash
those years Mom worked three jobs

and I went east. We shoe the grass
beside the old apartment. He asks again
whether the car's plow into a palm tree

or the heart attack killed our stepfather,
and what of those postmortem letters
dropped through the slot? The rhinoceros

no longer is horned; nothing left
to harvest. Those years have bowed
to the earth. We pluck fuchsia
blossoms we never knew grew here,
scatter smashed petals down the walk.

Listening to Charles Bernstein Read Essays While I Have a Migraine

Bernstein aura pulses as he damns convention.
My poems have lips and slip across bodies, my poems
would bore him, my brain paints him in glow-motion,
my brain wants him to be my friend, to like my poems.

In another field we cross-leg with Coleridge,
bees licking clover by our feet and hands,
we all smoke pipes, we are friends.

In another field Bernstein scribbles love poems
unironically, and Penn is a friendly place,
and it is 1973, it is 1805, it is 2078, and poetry
does not work only one job, and poetry

is a daisy chain in the grass left to be discovered,
and we all stick our fingers in, and we are all Jews
in the expanded field, and we all lie in the grass

weaving daisy chains, and Coleridge always lies
with us barefoot, and Bernstein pulses pulses pulses
as my eyes close, as my body lifts, as my legs carry me out
into blinding orange sun, weeping and stumbling into late late sun.

Blue Crab

for Elizabeth Catanese

And what if T. S. Eliot had been a crab
            scuttling across the ocean floor?
No sinister greased middle-part, no shovel
            to bury Shakespeare, that possible
imposter? But maybe the Earl
            of Oxford did bleed his longings
into those sonnets, Hamlet, Desdemona,
            and maybe Eliot should have been
a blue crab: no yellow fog, no women talking
            Michelangelo. To think he could have been
an ordinary poet, like all crabs,
            pincering out meter in Joe Fruscione's lucky
busted up trap or sizzling his love
            song in red broth, Baltimore crockpot—
scuttling iambic, trochaic in death.

Kansas

Overhead a boy shark
thrashed

in Tylosaurus proriger's
grip, tailfin

blasting brown-gold algae
through tropical water

in a time before hours
in a now vanished sea.

Listen with me
how the ground thrums

these warm Cretaceous
secrets. Cheek the chalky

dust. Hip the yellow
grass. Eons ago

a dark body buckled within
a more powerful body.

Eons ago my breathless
headlights cheeked your midnight

street.   Listen as if
what thrashes within

untouchable hours would speak
within invisible sea.

On Encountering William Blake's Head in Talissa Ford's Office

Talissa blames his apparent anger
on nose straws placed before the plaster set
into sunken cheek and lip, the strain

of narrow breath immortalized
in the dead poet's life mask. Our four hands
splay across his baldness

as she passes him; the weight startles.
He could be my stepfather, eyes closed
above the fading body folded

deep in an orange vinyl chair.
I slip fingers into a rough crack
in his neck, cradled

in my lap. His jowl and brow hairs
take my breath. She has another
of him at home, she says, intact.

On the Runaway Angus Bull the Stewarts Kindly Saved

One day he bellowed at inspection,
white face swinging above black hide,
so the clipboard marked him
for slaughter. Who knows what lit in him
then, or why. Maybe the previous day's forced
fucking, the inspector's prodding. He was a bull
of soft snorts, really, & of barnyard nuzzles
with cows he crushed on or those mourning
their young. The truck left much to be desired:
scant air, his body crammed humid & rough
against the bristled fur of his brethren
while the roaring rocked & threw them, buckling
their legs, banging them this way & that
in puddled urine & shit. It's hard to explain
the muscle that tightens in the throat
when a body knows now-or-never closes in.
The truck stopped near York College, Queens.
The air tasted of grass as the doors gave,
& he bolted down the street like a bull
whose bones had just felt pre-shocks of death.
He bolted past cars, across the college lawn,
lips open, hooves flinging wet earth
as humans pointed. A few circled. He dizzied,
however soothing they made their animal
voices. By a tree he staggered then.

Miriam, I remember

that August, muggy St. Louis,
when sleepless on stab-springed daybed, I crept,
3 a.m., for beer. Aging bare bulb that flickered & dimmed,
you hunched over letters, lithium-drugged, wavy hair cropped,
shoes strapped, nerves jilting shoulders
below hum-mumble & tongue click.

Two decades, I'd daydreamt your upright piano,
your feet for running everywhere,
your typing fingers,
your squeal of a laugh,
your loud tears,
your bruised arms,
your I never wanted your father—
what you never quite called rape.

Miriam, years later, at the dying facility
off the Missouri county highway,
when you remembered
nothing of your luscious body
or how faucets work
or your lightning words,
but you finally saw me,

loved me with my name,
all the fallow bells in me
scorched peals through my veins—

　　so fuck poisoned tongues, bipolar
legacy; to hell with gnarled memory, gritted
agony; goddamn violence, volatility, prescribed peace.
Your eyes sang me the churned sweet
of gentle release,
& mine sang back, holy grandmother, bone-rattled heat.

17

In the Beginning

The longer your beard, the softer
I heard your father's voice
as he finger-brushed your hair,
eyes closed, tickling your
mother's belly while you,
tiny astronaut, slept amid
her body's stars. I believe
in the beginning, how it is
always shuffling backward,
how every brittle thing softens
in reverse. This fig leaf, stiff
as paper, once knew how to be
small, potential, a speck of star.

The Light Is Flashing

I am the Jew who survived supernova,
whom gravity overwhelmed into contraction.

No light escaped for years.

I am the Jew of the schoolyard,
the chestnut Jew

whose body is made of stars.

I am the Jew who went nose shopping
in *Vogue* magazine at sixteen.

I am the Jew who recalls the metal file
grinding bone, the rectangled light
demonic through lids, the surgical mumbles

amid the radio. *Blame it on the black star,*
blame it on the falling sky, blame it on the satellite

that beams me home.

I am the 21st century Jew. I am the self-mocking Jew.
I am the Yiddish-faking, sh'ma stumbling,

wandering poet Jew.

When star-mass contracts to the size
of *Vogue*, I am the Jew who goes under twice

for skull-rattling scraping, bruised swelling,
itchy stitches, black eyes. The crowds

cheer, the crowds holler from behind barricades,
the light is flashing, and I am the Jew
sucking in the light and contracting,

I am the Jew days later ripping black threads
from her own face. I am the Jew

whose heart thumps inner ears,

having tripled the Vicodin

and aligned herself with the doorframe,

the Jew who thrusts herself face-first into its ridges,
splattering within them blood
that rains red onto white carpet.

Eli, Eli

Scattered embers, we long
for our ghost limbs made ash.

Ancient trunk, severed—
boughs incinerated—

and all those rings, concentric
knowledge, raw inside me, burning.

The Human Zoo

In the end, when cockroaches rule the land,
the few of us left will stretch
our glorious skin, naked and wingless,

across plastic boulders and AstroTurf
dampened by rusty spigots.

The cockroaches will stroll,
having paid in roach pheromone

for admission. On hairy legs
they'll hiss and whistle

as they gaze into cells littered
with moldy couches, busted laptops,

waterlogged tomes of Shakespeare.

When roaches swarm the Plexiglas,
we'll shriek, which they'll take for laughter.

Monkey fur will clump in the corner,
a monkey skull will gape from a phony pond,

and when we weep, they'll sway
and hold one another,
thinking it our mating song.

The Way of the Dodo

after David Quammen's The Song of the Dodo

Have you considered the knowledge
of that bird? How many centuries, probably
millennia, the dodo's large feet carried
her bottom-heavy bulk through Mauritian forests,
taught her young to use stones to digest
fruit and then, for those final decades,

to silence their anxious bodies when leaves
swished around human feet? The dodo
never would have named herself that
when her wings, softly feathered
& flightless, were full of such
breathy vowels, gentle consonants.

Maybe washewa or brathou—
Our dumb name began her annihilation,
inviting the Dutch to club her and her kind
and their kids whack-a-mole style, until
there was just one. Let's say she died
alone, wearied face tucked between

wide-leaved bushes, forgetful
of her features, not having a companion
to sing to for years beyond memory, as she
was the last holdout, escaped
from the men and their monkeys
and pigs, all alien to her world for uncountable

years. Maybe that's how the Colorado forgets
it's a river, named, as it was, for a color
the namers were already memorializing.
The West parches paler and paler tan, Los Angeles
desperate for water. What difference would it make
if the last dodo had had an unhatched son or daughter?

Fear Nothing

Our ancient irises, brown or blue-green
reservoirs of the Anthropocene's

last sunlit hours,

gather the days of Dreadnoughtus
through to the hours beyond us.

Invisible between our flickering faces,
tunnels of desire and pain.

Whatever breaks the hearts we hide
beckons unborn ghosts

to fleck amid brown or blue-green,

murmuring of futures
soaked with gasoline.

Kriah

The lake's been moaning
an earth-heavy groan
nightly, ice pushing
ice:

closed ears, listen.

Our goldenest word,
especially now—
heart contracting,
loosening, contracting—
is listen.

Mother is howling—
listen.

Notes

Redolence emerged from learning that Zyklon B reportedly smells of bitter almond.

Chaya Speaks references the poet's Hebrew name, Chaya Devorah; *Chaya* means "living" and is a root for the biblical name *Chava*, which is translated in English as *Eve*.

On the Runaway Angus Bull the Stewarts Kindly Saved refers to a rescue assisted by Jon and Tracey Stewart and covered by various news outlets in April 2016.

Eli, Eli is transliterated Hebrew meaning "my God, my God."

Kriah is the Jewish grief tradition of rending one's clothing.

Gratitude

This chapbook is offered in memory of my teacher and friend, Maxine Kumin.

Shout-out to the Get Fresh Crew and the rest of my Drew MFA family, especially to Roberto Carlos Garcia, whose faith in my work is the reason this chapbook opens in your hands. Mad love as well to Lisa Alexander, Cara Armstrong, Mary Brancaccio, Shaun Fletcher, Ysabel Gonzalez, Brett Haymaker, Peter Kirn, Lynne McEniry, Yesenia Montilla, Sean Morrissey, Heidi Sheridan, Marisa Frasca Patinella, and Sosha Nicole Pinson. And to Michelle Greco, Elliott batTzedek, Lori Wilson, David Crews, Jim Spears, Laurie Ann Guerrero, Rebecca Gayle Howell, and the late Monica Hand—and every Drew poet I ever deeply hugged—thank you for being at the invisible workshop table in my mind and often the real table at which we worked some of these poems. The MFA was a passport to a feast that never ends. To each of you, thank you.

Gratitude to mentors and teachers, many of whom have become beloved friends: Ross Gay, Aracelis Girmay, Joan Larkin, Anne Marie Macari, Jane Mead, Mihaela Moscaliuc, Sean Nevin, Alicia Ostriker, Mario Padilla, Patrick Rosal, Ira Sadoff, Angela Shaw, Gerald Stern, Jean Valentine, Judith Vollmer, Michael Waters, Ellen Dore Watson, and of course Max.

To other friends who inspired or offered guidance with this work, love and gratitude: Ann Cleveland, Ken Lacovara, Jean Lacovara, JC Todd, Charlie Manis, Elizabeth White Vidarte, Chris Schaeffer, Talissa Ford—and to Talissa's whole Romanticism and Extinction class at Temple University. To dear ones whose support sings my heart, thank you: Melissa Orner, Ann Brown, Lana Gold, Holly Perry, Jody Cohen, Vanessa Loh, Elli Kim, Dana Gehling, Liz Lachman, Gloria Willis, Sierra Fisk. Thank you, dear poets and friends in Castine, Philly, and LA; my Bryn Mawr sisters; my Temple colleagues and professors; and you for being here.

This collection wouldn't exist without my writing partner, collaborator, and dearest friend, poet and artist Elizabeth Catanese, who not only read every draft of these poems but often sat across the table while first drafts were born. E, your belief in these poems and in me has been bubbles, unicorns, Big Gay Ice Cream, LBI, Wizard of Oz: everything. Thank you.

To my mother, Barbara Ann, whose unconditional love and support and whose unmatched intelligence inspire me every day, thank you. To my father, Charles, whose wit and wild curiosity inform some of these poems, thank you. To my workout-buddy brother, Darren; my spunky artist sister, Vanessa; and my clever nephew, Miles (coconut!): your love sustains me. Thank you. Gratitude to Addie for keeping my lap warm, Whitman for keeping my face wet, and the late Mark for filling my writing space with joy and tumbling books. To the child to come: thank you for someday reading these poems, and for holding them.

To Betsy Reese, my favorite scientist, hilarious storyteller, creative thinker, historian—my beloved romancer and partner and sweetheart of a wife: thank you. This life with you is everything. I never knew it could be this good. I am the luckiest.

About the Poet

Darla Himeles, a Philadelphia-based poet, translator, and essayist, can be read in recent issues of *Women's Review of Books, American Poetry Review, Storyscape, New Ohio Review,* and Pittsburgh Poetry Review. An associate editor for *The Stillwater Review,* Darla holds an AB in English from Bryn Mawr College and an MFA in poetry and poetry in translation from Drew University. She is currently a doctoral student in American literature at Temple University.

CPSIA information can be obtained
at www.ICGtesting.com
Printed in the USA
LVHW110545130123
737041LV00004B/670